Building

Fireproof Teens

A Young Person's Guide to I Corinthians

James J. Burkc

Fireproof Commentaries

FIREPROOF
COMMENTARIES

Building Fireproof Teens: A Young Person's Guide to I Corinthians

© 2025 James J. Burke

Scripture quotations are from the King James Version (KJV) of the Bible.

Published by Fireproof Commentaries

Marinette, Wisconsin

fireproofcommentaries.org

ISBN: 979-8-9941637-3-3

Printed in the United States of America

Table of Contents

Session 1 – Faith on Fire in Corinth

Welcome to Corinth

Imagine stepping off a ship into a city louder and flashier than Las Vegas, more crowded than New York, and as diverse as TikTok's For You page. You see sailors unloading goods, athletes training for the Isthmian Games, politicians making deals, merchants selling idols, and priests leading people into marble temples. Gold coins jingle, perfume hangs in the air, music spills out of taverns, and voices shout in a dozen languages.

This is Corinth — the city where Paul planted a church. For teens living there, temptation lurked on every street corner. Corinth was famous for its wealth, sports, and especially for its immorality. It was a place where fame and pleasure ruled, and where living for Christ was a radical choice.

Sound familiar? Your world may not have marble temples, but it has its own idols — likes, followers, sports glory, and the pressure to fit in. Corinth's temptations mirror today's social media culture, high school hallways, and Friday-night scenes. The good news: the same Jesus who sustained the believers in Corinth can empower you too.

The Church in the Furnace of Corinth

Corinth was a major crossroads of the Roman Empire, rebuilt by Julius Caesar about a century before Paul arrived. With harbors on both sides of the isthmus, it was a trade capital. It also became a moral melting pot. Greek philosophy, Roman law, Eastern mysticism, and every vice imaginable found a home there.

Paul arrived after a rough stretch. In Acts 18 we read he came "in weakness, and in fear, and in much trembling" (1

Corinthians 2:3). He wasn't a celebrity preacher with a travel team and a book deal. He was a scarred missionary who had been beaten, mocked, and chased from city to city. Yet in Corinth, God gave him courage. He met Priscilla and Aquila, worked making tents, and started sharing the gospel.

Within months, a church sprang up — ordinary people rescued out of extraordinary sin. Former idol-worshipers, ex-slaves, merchants, and Roman citizens all gathered to worship Jesus. This was a miracle in a city like Corinth.

Paul begins his letter:

> *"Unto the church of God which is at Corinth, to them that are sanctified in Christ Jesus, called to be saints..." (1 Corinthians 1:2, KJV).*

Right away Paul calls them "sanctified" — set apart, holy — even though the rest of the letter will correct their immaturity. Why? Because their identity was not in their past but in Christ.

Sanctified:

Set apart by God and changed by Him to live more like Jesus—cleaned up on the inside and guided to live a life that honors Him.

Key truths for teens:

1. **Identity Comes First**. Before dealing with behavior, Paul affirms their identity. You are "in Christ." This is the root of everything else.

2. **Unity Is Non-Negotiable**. Corinth's church was divided by cliques ("I am of Paul," "I am of Apollos"). Paul insists Jesus is the only foundation (1 Corinthians 3:11).

3. **God Uses Weakness**. Paul didn't show up with flash; he showed up with faith. God's power works best in humble vessels.

For a teen today, these truths hit home:

- You're more than your social media bio.

- Don't get caught in popularity cliques.

- God can use your small efforts in big ways.

When you think of Corinth, think "hot furnace." Paul writes like a builder instructing workers: use gold, silver, and precious stones, not wood, hay, and stubble. What survives fire? Not the flashy stuff but what's solid.

Summary: Called to Be Saints

- **Your Identity**: You belong to Jesus first — not your school, your sports team, your online persona, or your friend group.

- **Your Mission:** Live holy lives in an unholy world, shining like lights in the dark.

- **Your Unity**: Don't let cliques or drama split the body of Christ.

- **Your Hope**: God's power shows up when you feel weak or overlooked.

When Paul called the Corinthians "saints," he wasn't flattering them. He was reminding them who they already were in Christ. And that's what this book — and this session — is about: building a fireproof life and a fireproof church by living out your true identity in Christ.

Application: Building Fireproof Faith

If Corinth were your school:

- Half your friends would be chasing new trends.

- A few would be trying to "go viral" at any cost.

- Some would mock you for your faith.

- Others would secretly hope you'd show them something real.

Paul's message to you: you're called to be different – but together.

1. **Living Set Apart**. Being sanctified doesn't mean acting superior. It means letting Christ shape your choices. Ask: "Will this action survive the fire?"

2. **Unity Over Cliques**. Whether it's sports teams, social groups, or youth group subgroups, remember Jesus is the foundation. Guard your heart against gossip, jealousy, and competition.

3. **God's Power in Weakness**. You don't have to be the loudest Christian on campus. Sometimes the quiet, faithful witness speaks louder than flashy words.

6

Practical ideas for teens:

- Start your day with Scripture before social media.

- Pray for classmates by name.

- Refuse to spread rumors.

- When pressured to compromise, remember your identity.

- Invite a friend to youth group or church.

When you choose to live fireproof, you're not just protecting yourself. You're becoming a living example to others. In Corinth, the believers' faith turned heads. In your world, it can do the same.

Activities & Discussion

Icebreaker: Show photos of cities like New York or Las Vegas. Ask students: "Where would it be hardest to be a Christian?" Transition: "That's Corinth."

Discussion Questions:

1. What's one way Corinth was like our world today?

2. Why do you think Paul calls them saints before correcting them?

3. What does "building with gold, silver, and precious stones" look like in your life?

4. Where do you feel pressure to fit in at school or online?

5. How could you build unity in your youth group this week?

Group Activity: Corinth Map. Show Corinth on a map of Greece. Highlight the two harbors and temples. Ask: "If you were Paul walking into this city, how would you feel?"

Unity Challenge: This week, intentionally reach out to someone in your group you don't know well. Pray with them or simply encourage them.

Memory Puzzle: Write 1 Corinthians 1:2 on slips of paper (one phrase per slip). Mix them up and have teens put it back in order.

Memory Verse

1 Corinthians 1:2 (KJV):

"Unto the church of God which is at Corinth, to them that are sanctified in Christ Jesus, called to be saints..."

Leader's Notes

Talk about what "sanctified" means: set apart for God's use. Encourage students to memorize it this week.

Prayer

"Lord Jesus, thank You for calling us to be saints in a world that pulls us in every direction. Give us courage like Paul had, unity like the early church, and a love that stands out. Help our lives to be built of things that last forever. In Jesus' name, Amen."

Leader's Notes

- **Object Lesson:** Bring two small items — one paper (burns easily), one metal (endures fire). Talk about which one you want your life to resemble.

- **Reinforce Identity**: Teens may feel shame or insecurity. Emphasize Paul starts with identity ("saints") before behavior.

- **Visual Aids**: A photo of ruins of Corinth or the temple of Apollo.

- **Engagement Tip**: Split students into two teams for verse activities to build excitement and memorization.

Session 2 – The Only Foundation

Who's on Your Team?

Imagine you're a coach building a team. Some players show up eager to play; others wear the jersey but never learn the game. They spend practices looking at their phones or talking about the latest gossip. When it's go time, they roll in late and are more focused on getting clout for the 'Gram than actually scoring points. You can't win championships with people who aren't truly committed.

Paul had the same concern for the church in Corinth. He wasn't just warning about building with bad habits — he was warning about building with people who weren't truly part of Christ. The foundation is Jesus. The "building materials" are the people we gather. If we fill the church with people who only act like Christians but haven't trusted Christ, the structure will fail when tested.

Teens face this too: you can be around church, youth group, and Christian music but not be personally committed to Christ. Paul's lesson: make sure you're the real deal and build friendships with those who are truly following Jesus.

The Only Foundation, The Right Materials

Paul writes:

> *"For other foundation can no man lay than that is laid, which is Jesus Christ" (1 Corinthians 3:11, KJV).*

When Paul talks about "gold, silver, and precious stones," don't picture jewelry or tiny gems. Think of the massive blocks of marble and granite you see in big public buildings—cut straight from the quarry, polished, and ready to last for centuries. God wants your life to be like that: strong, shaped on purpose, and built into something that endures. The opposite is wood, hay, and stubble—quick fixes, scrap lumber, or even the straw workers shove into gaps just to fill space. It looks like it's doing a job, but it burns up or blows away the moment a test comes. In real life, you can choose to be like that marble block—showing up, letting God shape you, getting stronger over time—or like the filler material that's just "there" but never built to last. Following Christ as a teen isn't about just "filling a spot" at youth group or church; it's about letting Him carve you, polish you, and set you into a place where your life makes a real, lasting impact.

Key truths for teens:

1. **Christ Is the Foundation**. You can't build a church or a life on anyone else. No pastor, parent, or influencer can save you.

2. **The Materials Are People**. Gold, silver, precious stones = people truly born again, built on Christ.

Wood, hay, stubble = people who look the part but don't know Him.

3. **Fire Tests Reality**. The "fire" represents God's judgment. Only those truly in Christ survive. This isn't about losing rewards; it's about revealing who belongs to Christ.

4. **Leaders Must Build Carefully**. Paul's warning is especially for leaders: don't rush to fill the church with numbers over genuine discipleship. But it's also a warning for teens: don't just "hang around" church — become the real deal.

For teens today:

You may grow up in a Christian home, go to a Christian school, or attend youth group — but unless you've personally trusted Christ, you're not going to last. When the fires of temptation, pressure or persecution come, you will burn away.

Persecution:

Unfair mistreatment because of who you are or believe.

Summary: Make Sure You're the Real Deal!

- Christ Is the Only Foundation.

- True Disciples Are the Building.

- Testing Will Reveal Reality.

- Your Choice Matters: Are you a true follower or just attending?

Paul's point: The church isn't a club; it's God's temple. Being "around" doesn't make you "in." Just as a fake brick will crumble in a fire, a person without Christ can't stand in judgment.

Application: Be Real, Build Real

Think about your closest circle of friends at church or school. Some are on fire for God; some are just tagging along. That was Corinth too. Paul's warning: choose authenticity.

✓ **Check Your Own Foundation**. Have you personally repented and trusted Jesus? Or are you riding on family or church culture?

✓ **Build Relationships with Real Believers**. Your inner circle matters. Surround yourself with people who truly love Jesus.

✓ **Don't Confuse Activity with Salvation**. Singing, volunteering, or wearing the T-shirt doesn't save you. Christ does.

✓ **Don't Be Afraid of Testing**. Peer pressure, temptation, or crisis may reveal who's real. Welcome it as God's way of making your faith genuine.

Practical tips:

- Write your own testimony — how you came to Christ — and share it with a friend.

- Ask God to show you if there's an area of your life you're faking.

- Pray for courage to stand even if friends fall away.

Activities & Discussion

Icebreaker: Build a tower with mixed materials — some sturdy (wood blocks), some flimsy (paper cups). Add weight or shake it. Watch which parts collapse. Discuss how this illustrates true vs. false converts.

Discussion Questions:

1. What does it mean to have Christ as your foundation personally?

2. Why do you think Paul compares people to building materials?

3. How can you tell if someone is truly following Jesus? (What fruit should we look for?)

4. How do peer pressure and trials reveal who's real?

5. Are you confident you're "gold" in God's building or just "hay" on the edge?

Group Activity: Testimony Pair-Up. Pair students to share their personal testimony in 2 minutes. This reinforces genuine faith and shows where someone may still have questions.

Unity Project: Encourage each student to pray for one peer by name who's on the fence spiritually.

Memory Challenge: Write 1 Corinthians 3:11 on the board and erase words as students recite it from memory.

Memory Verse

> *1 Corinthians 3:11 (KJV):*
>
> *"For other foundation can no man lay than that is laid, which is Jesus Christ."*

Leader's notes

Emphasize that only those built on this foundation survive testing.

Prayer

"Father, You have established the Lord Jesus as our only foundation. Help me to know You personally and to build my friendships and church life with people who are truly Yours. Reveal any area where I'm pretending. Make me real. Give me courage to stand when trials come. In Jesus' name, Amen."

Leader's Notes

- **Illustration Idea:** Bring two bricks — one solid, one crumbly — or a gold-painted stone vs. real stone.

- **Teaching Tip:** Emphasize salvation by grace, not works. Don't scare but do challenge teens to be sure.

- **Visual Aid:** Draw a foundation labeled "Christ" and two kinds of materials — "true believers" vs. "false professors."

- **Discussion Prompt:** Gently ask students to reflect privately on whether they've trusted Christ.

- **Memory Verse Drill:** Repeat 1 Corinthians 3:11 as a group, taking away words.

Session 3 – Servants and Stewards

Not the Celebrity Pastor

Think of your favorite athlete, influencer, or artist. They get thousands of likes and fans. Now imagine a coach or teacher who works quietly behind the scenes — no crowds, no hype — but actually trains and helps the athletes succeed.

Servants of Christ, Stewards of Mysteries

Back in Corinth, church life started to look like a popularity contest. Some were saying, "I'm Team Paul," others, "I'm Team Apollos," and still others, "I'm Team Cephas." They were treating their leaders like celebrities, measuring greatness by style and hype instead of character. But Paul shut that down. He wrote back, "We're just servants. Don't worship us." That sounds a lot like what Jesus taught: in God's kingdom, the greatest isn't the one with the biggest crowd or the flashiest profile — it's the one who humbly serves. Jesus said, "Whoever wants to be great must be your servant" and "the one who wants to be first must become the least" (see Matthew 20:26-28). Real leadership isn't about collecting followers or likes; it's about pointing people to Christ, helping them grow, and doing the hard work behind the scenes without needing the spotlight.

For teens, this is huge: your world says "Be famous." Jesus says "Be faithful." Instead of chasing clout, He calls you to be a steward — a trusted caretaker of something that belongs to God.

Paul writes:

> *"Let a man so account of us, as of the ministers of Christ, and stewards of the mysteries of God. Moreover it is required in stewards, that a man be found faithful"* (1 Corinthians 4:1-2, KJV).

Key truths for teens:

1. **Ministers = Servants.** The Greek word is literally "under-rowers" — like slaves rowing a ship. Paul and Apollos were not bosses but rowers pulling in sync with Christ.

2. **Stewards = Managers of Someone Else's Property.** A steward managed a household for the master. He didn't own it but protected it and grew it. Teens today are stewards of time, talents, influence, friendships.

3. **Faithfulness > Flashiness.** Paul says God evaluates us on faithfulness, not fame. Likes, awards, and applause don't impress Him. Quiet consistency does.

4. **God Is the Judge.** Paul warns against judging too early. We don't know hearts. God will reveal hidden motives at the right time.

5. **Humility Protects Unity.** By reminding the Corinthians their leaders were just servants, Paul dismantled the cult of personality and protected the church's unity.

Key truths for teens:

1. Don't turn Christian leaders into idols.

2. Don't measure yourself by followers or applause.

3. Remember God entrusted you with gifts to use for Him.

Summary: Faithfulness Over Fame

- **Servants Not Stars:** Christian leaders (and you) are called to serve, not be celebrities.

- **Stewards of God's Stuff:** Everything you have — time, talent, money, opportunities — belongs to God.

- **Faithfulness Required:** God measures consistency, not flash.

- **God Judges Motives:** Stop comparing and start serving.

When Paul wrote these words, he was pulling the Corinthian church back from personality cults and competition. Teens can learn the same lesson early and avoid a lifetime of chasing empty applause.

Application: Living as God's Steward

In a world of TikTok, Instagram, and YouTube, it's easy to believe your value comes from views. Paul says your value comes from being Christ's servant.

- Recognize Your Stewardship. List your gifts: skills, friendships, resources, even your social media. All belong to God.

- Choose Faithfulness Daily. It's not about the big moment. It's about showing up: reading Scripture, praying, helping a friend, serving at church, telling the truth.

- Stop Comparing. Someone else's platform doesn't diminish your assignment. God called you to your lane.

- Use Small Opportunities Well. If you're faithful with little, God can trust you with more. That starts now, not "someday when I'm an adult."

- Welcome Accountability. Let mentors or leaders ask you how you're doing spiritually. This keeps your heart steady and humble.

Ask yourself this week:

- What's one area I've been chasing applause instead of faithfulness?

- How can I serve someone quietly this week?

- Who can I trust to hold me accountable?

Activities & Discussion

Icebreaker: Show two photos: a celebrity influencer and a backstage stagehand or coach. Ask: "Who's more valuable?" Discuss how hidden faithfulness can matter more than visible fame.

Discussion Questions:

- What does it mean to be a "servant of Christ" as a teen?

- How are you a "steward" right now?

- Why do you think God values faithfulness over fame?

- How can accountability help you stay humble?

- What's a small way you could serve quietly this week?

Group Activity: Stewardship Inventory. Have students make a quick list of what God has entrusted to them (talents, time, friends). Then pray over the list, asking God to help them be faithful stewards.

Quiet Challenge: Encourage each teen to do one unseen act of service this week and report back (if comfortable) next time.

Memory Game: Write 1 Corinthians 4:2 on cards and scramble them. Have teams assemble the verse in order.

Memory Verse

1 Corinthians 4:2 (KJV):

"Moreover it is required in stewards, that a man be found faithful."

Leader's Note

Encourage students to memorize it and ask: "What does faithful look like for you?"

Prayer

"Lord Jesus, help us remember we're Your servants, not stars. Everything we have belongs to You. Make us faithful stewards of our time, talents, and friendships. Protect us from pride and comparison. Give us joy in serving You quietly and consistently. In Jesus' name, Amen."

Leader's Notes

- **Illustration Idea:** Bring a broom or service tool —
something humble but necessary — to illustrate unseen
faithfulness.

- **Teaching Tip:** Teens may confuse faithfulness with
boredom. Remind them God sees hidden service and
rewards it.

- **Visual Aid:** Draw a ship with rowers underneath and
a captain above to show "under-rowers."

- **Accountability Cue:** Encourage small groups or
pairs for ongoing check-ins.

- **Memory Verse Drill:** Have students chant
"Faithfulness over fame" as they repeat 1 Corinthians
4:2.

Session 4 – Living Pure in a Polluted World

Contagion

Picture a loaf of bread rising on the counter. It starts as a lump of dough, but when you mix in yeast, the yeast spreads until the whole lump is puffed up. Or imagine a glass of clean water with just one drop of dye — within minutes the whole glass is tinted.

A little leaven leaveneth the whole lump." – 1 Corinthians 5:6

Paul used that same idea in 1 Corinthians 5. He told the Corinthian church: a little leaven leavens the whole lump. In other words, a little tolerated sin spreads and harms everyone.

Teens know this from experience. One toxic friend can sour an entire friend group. One bad TikTok trend can sweep through a school in days. Purity matters not just for you but for your community.

Paul's call is clear: Christ makes us unleavened — clean. Don't let sin back in.

Purity and Discipline in the Church

Paul writes:

> "Know ye not that a little leaven leaveneth the whole lump? Purge out therefore the old leaven, that ye may be a new lump, as ye are unleavened. For even Christ our passover is sacrificed for us" (1 Corinthians 5:6-7, KJV).

Paul warned the Corinthians that letting sin slide wasn't compassion — it was actually harmful. They thought they were being "open-minded" or "tolerant," but they were really letting something poisonous spread. Celebrating sin in the name of tolerance isn't real love; real love wants what's best for someone, even if that means hard conversations or unpopular choices. Jesus said His followers are meant to be the "salt of the earth" and the "light of the world" (Matthew 5:13–16) — salt keeps things from rotting and light helps people see clearly. In the same way, God calls His people to holiness not to ruin our fun but to protect us, guide us, and help us thrive. When we ignore or cheer on harmful behavior, we're not helping the person who's stuck in it — we're leaving them in danger. But when we shine God's light and call each other back to His ways, we're acting out of true love, because holiness leads to freedom, healing, and a stronger, healthier church family for everyone.

Paul also reminded the Corinthians that his correction was aimed at people inside the church — God's family — not at outsiders. We shouldn't be shocked when people who don't know Jesus live like they don't know Jesus. Lost people are going to live lost lives. Our job isn't to police the world but to shine Christ's light and show His love so they can be drawn to Him. Inside the church, though, we've already said "Jesus is Lord," so we hold each other to a different standard. That's why correction is about family care, not public shaming — we're helping our brothers and sisters stay healthy and strong in their walk with Christ while showing the world a better way to live.

Key truths for teens:

1. **Sin Spreads.** Paul uses yeast (leaven) to describe how even a small compromise can affect the whole group.

2. **We Are Unleavened in Christ.** Because of Christ's sacrifice, God sees us as clean. Therefore, we live like who we are.

3. **Discipline Is Love.** Removing leaven wasn't cruelty; it was protection. Just like a doctor removes infection, the church protects its members by dealing with sin.

4. **Witness Is at Stake.** The world watches how believers handle sin. If we ignore it, we tarnish Christ's name.

5. **Personal Purity Fuels Corporate Health.** The church's strength comes from individuals who live holy lives.

For teens today:

- Tolerating sin in your life weakens your witness.

- Your private choices impact your youth group's power.

- Accountability isn't legalism; it's love.

Paul's Passover reference reminds them of Exodus: Israel had to remove leaven before the feast. Leaven = old life. Christ = our Passover Lamb. Because He died, we live clean.

Summary: Holy People in an Unholy World

- **Sin Spreads:** Even a little tolerated sin damages the whole group.

- **You Are Clean:** Christ has already made you unleavened — live like it.

- **Discipline Protects:** God's rules aren't to hurt you but to help you.

- **Witness Matters:** The world takes cues from your life.

Paul's message: holiness isn't a rulebook; it's a reflection of who you already are in Christ. Purity protects your joy, your friendships, and your testimony.

Application: Practicing Purity

1. **Check Your Heart.** Ask: Is there "leaven" — sin or compromise — in my life that I'm tolerating? This could be secret habits, dishonest behavior, or toxic media.

2. **Guard Your Inputs.** What you watch, listen to, and scroll through shapes your heart. Leaven can sneak in through your phone.

3. **Choose Friends Who Strengthen You.** Bad company corrupts good morals (1 Corinthians 15:33). Seek friends who help you grow in Christ.

4. **Be Accountable.** Have a mentor or friend you can be honest with. This protects you from secret sin.

5. **Respond Right to Discipline.** If a leader or parent confronts you in love, don't resist. See it as God's care.

6. **Live as Unleavened.** You're already forgiven in Christ. Live clean not to earn His love but because you have His love.

Practical Ideas for Teens:

- Clean out your "feed" like Israel cleaned out leaven before Passover. Unfollow or delete what tempts you.

- Pray Psalm 139:23–24 asking God to search your heart.

- Pick one area to "detox" this week — maybe a type of music, show, or online habit.

Ask yourself this week:

- What's one area of compromise I need to address?

- How could I support a friend who's struggling without judging them?

- How can our youth group maintain a pure witness?

Activities & Discussion

Icebreaker: Bring a small amount of food coloring and drip it into a clear cup of water. Watch it spread. Connect this to how sin spreads.

Discussion Questions:

- Why do you think Paul compares sin to yeast?

- What does it mean to be "unleavened" in Christ?

- How can we show love when someone is in sin?

- Why is purity so important to the church's witness?

- How can accountability be done without shaming?

Group Activity: Purity Inventory. Have students write down (privately) one area where they want to "clean out the leaven." Have them pray silently, then shred or discard the paper as a sign of leaving it behind.

Unity Challenge. Pair students to pray for each other's purity during the week.

Memory Challenge. Write 1 Corinthians 5:7 on the board and erase words each time as students recite it from memory.

Memory Verse

1 Corinthians 5:7 (KJV):

"Purge out therefore the old leaven, that ye may be a new lump, as ye are unleavened. For even Christ our passover is sacrificed for us."

Leader's Note

Explain that this verse ties personal holiness to Christ's sacrifice.

Prayer

"Lord Jesus, thank You for being our Passover Lamb. You have made us clean. Help us live pure in a polluted world. Show us any hidden leaven and give us the courage to remove it. Protect our youth group's witness and fill us with love for holiness. In Jesus' name, Amen."

Leader's Notes

- **Illustration Idea:** Bring a little yeast and dough to show how leaven works, or a video of dough rising. Keep checking it throughout the session.

- **Teaching Tip:** Teens may equate purity with shame. Emphasize identity ("you are unleavened") before behavior.

- **Visual Aid:** Draw a loaf labeled "church" with arrows showing how leaven spreads.

- **Group Guidance:** If students confess struggles, handle with grace and point them to Christ, not punishment.

- **Memory Verse Drill:** Erase words gradually or do a call-and-response reading to lock it in.

Session 5 – Handle Conflict God's Way

The Schoolyard Fight

Think about the last time you saw a big blow-up at school or online. Maybe two friends were fighting in the hallway, or an argument went viral on social media. People pick sides, rumors fly, screenshots spread, and within hours everyone knows. Even when the conflict started small, it escalated into a public mess.

Christians and Conflict

The Corinthians were doing the same thing — only worse. Instead of working out their disagreements inside the church, they were suing each other in public court. Paul couldn't believe it. He reminded them that believers are supposed to be saints who will one day judge the world — yet they couldn't even settle everyday arguments. Jesus had already taught in Matthew 18 that when someone hurts you, you should go to them privately first, then bring in a couple of trusted people if needed, and only involve the larger church as a last step. Paul's point was the same: God's people should solve problems with wisdom, humility, and forgiveness inside the family of faith, not air their dirty laundry in front of people who don't know Christ.

Jesus' teaching in Matthew 18 isn't just about rules — it's about healing relationships. After telling His followers how to handle conflict, He also told the parable of the unforgiving servant to show how important forgiveness is. The goal isn't to "win" the argument or punish someone; the goal is to restore your brother or sister and keep the family of God healthy. When someone repents, we forgive, just like God forgave us through Christ. Forgiveness doesn't mean pretending the hurt never happened — it means choosing to let go of revenge and giving the other person a chance to start fresh. This attitude turns conflict into an opportunity to show God's grace, which makes the church stronger and sets an example for the world watching from the outside.

Teens face conflict constantly — in friend groups, at school, on social media. Paul's lesson is clear: a fireproof life doesn't handle conflict like the world does. It forgives, reconciles, and keeps Christ's reputation first.

Paul writes:

> *"Dare any of you, having a matter against another, go to law before the unjust, and not before the saints?" (1 Corinthians 6:1, KJV).*

Background:

In Corinth, lawsuits were almost entertainment. Public courts were crowded, and people loved watching arguments. It was like reality TV. The Corinthian believers had absorbed that culture and were taking church disagreements into the public square.

Key truths for teens:

1. **God Expects His People to Solve Problems Differently.** Paul's outrage shows how serious it is when Christians mimic the world's fighting style.

2. **Saints Will Judge the World.** Paul argues from the future: one day you'll rule with Christ — can't you handle a small disagreement now?

3. **Lawsuits Damage the Church's Witness.** When Christians fight publicly, the world mocks. It undermines the gospel.

4. **Better to Be Wronged than to Harm the Body.** Paul says, "Why do ye not rather take wrong?" It's better to be cheated than to drag Christ's name through the mud.

5. **Conflict Tests Our Foundation.** How we respond to offenses shows whether we're building with genuine disciples or just church culture.

For teens today:

- Drama at school or in youth group spreads like wildfire.

- How you handle conflict shows your maturity in Christ.

- Forgiveness protects your witness and your peace.

Paul's warning is about the quality of the "building materials" — people. True believers will seek reconciliation; false professors thrive on conflict. As a teen, ask: am I a peacemaker or a drama-stirrer?

Summary: Peacemakers Not Plaintiffs

- Christians Don't Fight Like the World.

- Your Witness Matters More Than Winning.

- You're Called to Judge the World — Start Practicing Now.

Plaintiff:

The person who starts a lawsuit asking for help.

- Better to Take a Loss Than to Shame Christ's Name.

Paul's point: believers must handle disputes inside the family of God with humility and grace. This doesn't mean ignoring abuse or covering up crime — it means ordinary conflicts should be handled through reconciliation, not public shaming.

Living Out Peacemaking

Conflict is normal. How you respond is what sets you apart.

1. **Slow Down Before You React.** When you feel attacked or wronged, pause. Pray. Don't fire off that text or post.

2. **Go Directly, Not Publicly.** Jesus taught in Matthew 18 to go to the person privately first. Don't start with group chats or social media.

3. **Forgive Freely.** Paul says it's better to be wronged. Sometimes you choose to let it go rather than escalate.

4. **Seek Wise Help.** If you can't solve it alone, involve a mature leader, not the whole crowd.

5. **Check Your Motives.** Do you want justice, revenge, or reconciliation? God calls you to restore, not destroy.

6. **Protect Christ's Name.** Ask: "If an unbeliever watched how I handle this, would it honor Jesus?"

Practical Ideas for Teens:

- Role-play a conflict: one side offends, the other practices Matthew 18 steps.

- Write a prayer for a person you're upset with instead of gossiping about them.

- Practice giving the benefit of the doubt: assume misunderstanding, not malice.

Ask yourself this week:

- Do I handle conflict more like Corinth or like Christ?

- What's one current drama I can de-escalate?

- Who could mentor me in biblical conflict resolution?

Activities & Discussion

Icebreaker: Two volunteers act out a small disagreement (borrowed item not returned). Audience suggests ways to resolve it. Show how each approach either escalates or de-escalates the conflict.

Discussion Questions:

1. Why was Paul upset about lawsuits among believers?

2. What does it mean to "rather take wrong"?

3. How can Matthew 18 principles apply to our youth group?

4. Why does public fighting harm our witness?

5. How can forgiveness free you even if the other person isn't sorry?

Group Activity: Forgiveness Inventory. Ask students to write down (privately) a conflict or resentment. Pray over it. Then crumple or shred the paper as a symbol of releasing it to God.

Unity Project: Encourage each teen to do one secret act of kindness toward someone they've disagreed with.

Memory Challenge: Write 1 Corinthians 6:7 on the board and erase words gradually as students recite it.

Memory Verse

1 Corinthians 6:7 (KJV):

"Why do ye not rather take wrong? why do ye not rather suffer yourselves to be defrauded?"

Leader's Note

Encourage students to memorize it and discuss what it means to choose humility over winning.

Prayer

"Lord Jesus, teach us to handle conflict Your way. Forgive us for fighting like the world. Give us patience, humility, and courage to reconcile. Protect our youth group's witness and fill us with love that chooses unity over winning. In Jesus' name, Amen."

Leader's Notes

- **Illustration Idea:** Bring a sports jersey and a referee whistle. Show how staying in the "family" vs. going to "court" works.

- **Teaching Tip:** Teens need to hear that forgiveness isn't weakness. Frame it as strength and obedience.

- **Visual Aid:** Draw a courthouse vs. a cross to show worldly vs. Christlike conflict resolution.

- **Safety Note:** Make clear that abuse or crime should always be reported to authorities — this passage is about ordinary disputes.

- **Memory Verse Drill:** Role-play scenarios then recite the verse together to lock it in.

Session 6 – Honor God With Your Body

This House Is Not Yours

Imagine you're house-sitting for a friend. They've given you the keys to a beautiful home while they're away. You get to live there, but it's not yours. How would you treat it? Would you trash the living room or take care of it?

Paul says your body is like that. God designed it, Christ redeemed it, and the Holy Spirit lives in it. It's not really yours — it's God's temple. The Corinthians were living like their bodies didn't matter. Paul reminded them: "You are not your own; you were bought with a price."

Teens are bombarded with messages about body image, self-expression, and doing whatever "feels right." Paul flips that: your body is a sacred space, a holy place where God dwells. Honoring God with your body is not about shame but about dignity, value, and purpose.

Your Body Is a Temple

Paul writes:

> *"What? know ye not that your body is the temple of the Holy Ghost which is in you, which ye have of God, and ye are not your own? For ye are bought with a price: therefore glorify God in your body, and in your spirit, which are God's" (1 Corinthians 6:19-20, KJV).*

Corinth was a city of temples and slogans. Believers had been saved out of a culture that treated the body like a playground or a product. Some at Corinth even argued, "All things are lawful unto me" and "Meats for the belly, and the belly for meats," as if

the body were a temporary shell that didn't matter (cf. 6:12–13). Paul answers: your body matters to God—He created it, Christ redeemed it, and the Spirit indwells it. That is why he says, "What? know ye not that your body is the temple of the Holy Ghost... and ye are not your own? For ye are bought with a price... therefore glorify God in your body, and in your spirit, which are God's."

Two anchors: Indwelling and Ownership.

Paul gives two reasons that reshape everything we do with our bodies:

1. **Indwelling** — "Your body is the temple of the Holy Ghost." In the Old Testament, God's presence marked the temple as holy. Now, in Christ, God's presence lives in His people. A temple isn't common space; it is consecrated space. If the Holy Spirit lives in you, then what you do with your eyes, ears, mouth, hands, and feet happens in God's house. This isn't meant to shame you—it is meant to honor you. God calls your body a temple, not a mistake.

2. **Ownership** — "Ye are not your own... ye are bought with a price." Redemption means Jesus paid a real cost to make you His—not to erase your personhood, but to

set you free from sin's ownership and restore you to your true Owner. Belonging to Christ gives your body purpose and security. You are wanted, valued, and purchased at the cost of His blood. The right response to that love is worship with your whole self.

Why Paul talks about the body here.

Some Corinthians imagined a split between "spiritual life" and "physical life." Paul tears down that wall. Already in this paragraph he ties the body to (1) the Lord's purpose ("the body is for the Lord, and the Lord for the body," 6:13), (2) the resurrection ("God hath both raised up the Lord, and will also raise up us," 6:14), and (3) union with Christ ("your bodies are the members of Christ," 6:15). In other words, the body isn't disposable or unspiritual—it is part of your future glory, joined to Christ now, and destined for resurrection then. That's why what we do in the body matters.

Why sexual sin is "different."

Paul says, "Flee fornication. Every sin that a man doeth is without the body; but he that committeth fornication sinneth against his own body" (6:18). Sexual sin uniquely involves the body's one-flesh design and the heart's deepest bonds. It is not the only sin, and it is not the unforgivable sin, but it is uniquely violating because it misuses what God meant for covenant and witness.

Temple language.

Think of a temple's doors and rooms. Doors control what enters (eyes and ears) and what exits (words we say, actions we take). Inside, a temple is arranged for worship —not for trash storage. Guarding inputs (media, lyrics, images, substances) and outputs (speech, touch, behavior) is not legalism; it is temple care."Glorify God in your body, and in your spirit."

Paul refuses the fake choice between "spiritual" and "physical." Both belong to God. So glorifying God is whole-person worship:

- **Purity:** We flee what defiles the temple and pursue what fits the temple—truth, honor, and self-control.

- **Stewardship:** Sleep, nutrition, exercise, and modesty are not vanity projects; they're acts of gratitude to your Owner.

- **Service:** Hands that help, feet that go, a mouth that blesses—these are temple offerings that please the Lord.

None of this earns God's love; it flows from the price already paid and the Presence already given.

How grace motivates change.

Shame says, "Your body is dirty, so hide." Grace says, "Your body is holy because God lives here—so walk in dignity." The gospel supplies both pardon (Christ paid your price) and power (the Spirit indwells you). When teens fail—and honest disciples sometimes do—this passage invites them back to the One who owns them and lives in them. Confess, receive cleansing, and keep walking as God's temple.

How this builds a fireproof life.

Temples were built to last. When teens learn to see their bodies as God's dwelling, they start making decisions that endure the test of fire—honor over impulse, worship over trends, stewardship over self-harm, covenant over counterfeit intimacy. That is what a fireproof life looks like in the body.

Therefore...

"Ye are bought with a price: therefore glorify God in your body, and in your spirit, which are God's." This is not a small add-on to Christian life; it is a daily calling. Wherever a believer goes, a temple goes. Wherever a believer acts, worship can happen.

Key truths for teens:

1. **God Designed Your Body.** Psalm 139:14 says you're "fearfully and wonderfully made." Your body is not an accident.

2. **Christ Purchased Your Body.** The cross didn't just buy your soul. It bought all of you.

3. **The Holy Spirit Indwells Your Body.** You are now a mobile temple — God's presence goes where you go.

4. **Sexual Sin Is Different.** Paul says sexual immorality uniquely violates the body, which belongs to Christ. That's why boundaries matter.

5. **Glorify God With All of You.** What you eat, watch, wear, say, and do physically either honors or dishonors God.

For teens today:

- This affects choices about sex, substances, self-harm, and even self-talk.

- Honoring your body isn't about legalism — it's about living as God's temple.

- Purity and health aren't shame; they're stewardship.

Summary: Fireproof Temples

God Owns You: You're not your own; you're bought with a price.

God Lives in You: The Spirit indwells your body — you're sacred space.

Sin Profanes the Temple: What you allow in your body affects your worship.

Glorify God with All of You: This is dignity, not shame.

This reframes the body not as an object to manipulate or despise but as a place of honor, worship, and purpose.

Living as God's Temple

1. **Recognize Your Body's Value.** Don't let culture tell you you're "less than." God calls your body His temple.

2. **Guard Against Sexual Sin.** Paul's command to flee immorality still applies. Boundaries aren't outdated — they're protective.

3. **Steward Your Physical Health.** Sleep, nutrition, exercise — taking care of your body is part of honoring God.

4. **Avoid Substances or Habits That Harm.** Addictions or self-harm dishonor God's temple. Seek help and accountability if you struggle.

5. **Dress and Speak With Respect.** How you present yourself reflects your value. Modesty is not hiding but showing dignity.

6. **Renew Your Mind.** Your thoughts about your body matter too. Reject lies; embrace God's truth.

Practical ideas for teens:

- Create a "Temple Care" checklist with habits to honor God physically.

- Unfollow media that promotes harmful body image or temptation.

- Pray daily: "Lord, my body is Yours today."

Ask yourself this week:

- In what area am I dishonoring God with my body?

- How can I reclaim that area for Christ?

- Who could help me be accountable in my purity and health?

Activities & Discussion

Icebreaker: Show a photo of a famous temple or cathedral. Ask: "Would you spray graffiti on this?" Then connect to the body as God's temple.

Discussion Questions:

- Why do you think Paul calls your body a temple?

- How does knowing the Spirit lives in you change your decisions?

- What are practical ways to glorify God with your body?

- How does culture pressure teens to misuse their bodies?

- How can we support each other in living pure and healthy?

Group Activity: Temple Maintenance.

Have students brainstorm a "Temple Maintenance Plan" — daily/weekly practices that honor God physically, mentally, emotionally.

Unity Project: Pair students to pray for each other's purity and health during the week.

Memory Challenge: Write 1 Corinthians 6:19–20 on the board and erase words as students recite it.

Memory Verse

1 Corinthians 6:19-20 (KJV):

"What? know ye not that your body is the temple of the Holy Ghost which is in you, which ye have of God, and ye are not your own? For ye are bought with a price: therefore glorify God in your body, and in your spirit, which are God's."

Prayer

"Lord Jesus, thank You for making our bodies Your temples. Forgive us for treating them carelessly. Help us honor You with our thoughts, choices, and habits. Strengthen us to flee temptation and live with dignity. Let our lives show the world that You dwell in us. In Jesus' name, Amen."

Leader's Notes

Illustration Idea: Bring a small model of a church or temple. Ask how we treat sacred spaces, then connect to our bodies.

Teaching Tip: Emphasize dignity and ownership, not shame. Teens need positive motivation.

Visual Aid: Draw a temple labeled "Your Body" with doors representing eyes, ears, mouth, hands, feet. Discuss what enters/exits.

Group Guidance: Handle sensitive topics gently. Offer resources for students who struggle with self-harm or sexual sin. Make certain to stress that abuse is a sin and a crime and must be reported to authorities.

Memory Verse Drill: Have students write the verse in their journal, circling "temple," "Holy Ghost," and "bought with a price."

Session 7 – Bought With a Price

Whose Jersey Are You Wearing?

Imagine an athlete who's been traded to a new team but keeps wearing his old jersey. He attends the new team's practices, but on game day he runs out in the old colors. It confuses everyone — who does he belong to?

Paul tells the Corinthians: you're not your own anymore. Christ paid for you. You belong to Him now — body, mind, and spirit. Stop wearing the old jersey. Live like the team you're on.

For teens, identity can be confusing. Culture says "Be whoever you want." Christ says "I've bought you with a price — you're mine." This isn't control; it's love. The One who paid for you values you. When you understand that, your choices, your confidence, and your direction in life all change.

Identity Through Redemption

Paul writes:

> *"For ye are bought with a price: therefore glorify God in your body, and in your spirit, which are God's" (1 Corinthians 6:20, KJV).*

In Corinth, slavery was a fact of life. People could be bought and sold in the marketplace, either to be used or sometimes to be set free. Paul uses that familiar image to explain the gospel. He tells believers: Jesus has bought you. The price was not silver or gold—it was His own blood shed on the cross (1 Peter 1:18–19). But unlike human masters, Christ purchased us not to exploit but to liberate. He sets us free from sin's ownership and restores us to God's family.

That purchase changes everything about identity. Without Christ, people are shaped by whatever claims them— desires, culture, or peer opinion. Teens especially feel pulled to "be whatever you want," or to chase belonging through grades, sports, appearance, or popularity. But Paul insists: you are not your own. That's not a loss—it's security. You don't have to invent yourself or fight for a place in the world. You already belong to Christ, who calls you His treasured possession.

And here's where worth comes in. The world values people based on performance or image. Friends can change opinions overnight. Culture celebrates you one day and cancels you the next. But your worth is anchored in the price Christ paid. You were worth His life. That means your value isn't up for debate. No insult, no failure, no comparison can undo the fact that the Son of God gave Himself for you. The cross becomes the measure of your identity: deeply loved, infinitely valued, eternally secure.

Paul then commands: "Therefore glorify God in your body, and in your spirit." To glorify means to shine, to reflect God's greatness. Just as a mirror catches and reflects sunlight, your life reflects His character to the world. Your body—how you act, speak, dress, and treat others—becomes a living testimony of His holiness. Your spirit—your attitudes, desires, and loyalties—reveals His love and truth. Together, body and spirit form a whole-life response: show God's worth by the way you live.

So the logic is simple: You've been bought with the highest price. You belong to Christ. Your worth is fixed in His sacrifice. Now live in such a way that others can see His light shining through you—because your life isn't random anymore, it's radiant with purpose.

Key truths for teens:

1. You Were Slaves to Sin. Romans 6 says we were "servants of sin." We couldn't break free on our own.

2. Christ Paid the Ultimate Price. Not silver or gold but His own blood (1 Peter 1:18–19). That's how much you're worth.

3. You Belong to Him Now. Ownership has changed hands. You're under new management. This affects how you live, speak, and treat others.

4. Identity Shapes Behavior. The more you know you belong to Christ, the less you'll crave approval from peers or culture.

5. Glorify God With All You Are. Paul adds "body and spirit" — no compartments. Everything you are belongs to God.

For teens today:

- **You have value:** Christ shed His blood to purchase you

- **You have purpose:** Everything you are and have are to bring attention to your Father

- **You have security:** You're not drifting; you're owned and loved.

Summary: New Ownership, New Life

You Were Bought: Jesus paid for you with His life.

You're Not Your Own: Your plans, dreams, and choices now sit under His Lordship.

You're Valuable: The price shows your worth to God.

You're Secure: You belong forever.

Paul's point: Stop living as if you still belong to sin. Wear the jersey of Christ with joy.

Application: Living Like You're Bought

1. **Believe Your Worth.** God paid a cosmic price. Don't treat yourself cheaply or let others devalue you.

2. **Surrender Your Plans.** Since you belong to Christ, your goals, relationships, and habits go under His authority. Pray, "Lord, what do You want?"

3. **Refuse to Live in the Old Jersey.** Stop patterns that belong to your pre-Christ life. You're not that person anymore.

4. **Steward Your Gifts.** Everything you have — time, talent, influence — is now a trust from God. Use it wisely.

5. **Find Security in Belonging.** Peer pressure loses power when you're sure of Whose you are.

Practical Ideas for Teens:

- Write "Property of Jesus" at the top of a journal page. List areas of your life you're surrendering.

- Create a "New Jersey" art project — design a logo or jersey representing your identity in Christ.

- Pray daily: "Lord, I'm Yours. Live through me today."

Ask yourself this week:

- What area of my life am I still holding back from God?

- How does knowing I'm "bought" change my view of temptation?

- Who could I encourage this week about their worth in Christ?

Activities & Discussion

Icebreaker: Bring two jerseys (or T-shirts) from rival teams. Ask a volunteer to wear the "wrong" jersey. Discuss confusion and loyalty. Connect to belonging to Christ.

Discussion Questions:

- What does "bought with a price" mean to you personally?

- How does belonging to Christ change how you see yourself?

- Why does identity affect behavior?

- How does this truth free you from peer pressure?

- How can you remind yourself daily Whose you are?

Group Activity: Identity Contract.

Have students write a simple "contract" stating: "I belong to Jesus. I surrender _____." Then pray over it.

Unity Project: Encourage students to affirm each other's worth in Christ this week (notes, texts, encouragements).

Memory Challenge: Write 1 Corinthians 6:20 on the board and erase words gradually as students recite it.

☐

Memory Verse

1 Corinthians 6:20 (KJV):

"For ye are bought with a price: therefore glorify God in your body, and in your spirit, which are God's."

Leader's Note

Encourage students to memorize it and reflect on what it means to glorify God in both body and spirit.

Prayer

"Lord Jesus, thank You for paying the ultimate price for me. Help me live like I truly belong to You. Take every part of my life – body, mind, plans, dreams – and use them for Your glory. Make me secure in Your ownership and joyful in Your service. In Jesus' name, Amen."

Leader's Notes

- **Illustration Idea:** Bring a price tag or receipt — show how cost reflects value.

- **Teaching Tip:** Teens struggle with identity and worth. Emphasize belonging and love over control.

- **Visual Aid:** Draw two columns — "Old Owner" (sin) and "New Owner" (Christ). List differences.

- **Group Guidance:** Encourage students to talk privately with a leader if they have questions about salvation or surrender.

- **Memory Verse Drill:** Have students form a circle, each saying one word of the verse until it's complete.

Session 8 – Called to Live Content

The Waiting Room

Think about being in a waiting room at the doctor's office. You've got your number, you're scrolling your phone, but you're not really living — you're waiting. Many teens feel like life is one big waiting room: waiting to grow up, waiting to get a license, waiting to go to college, waiting to start dating, waiting for the "real" life to begin.

Paul writes to the Corinthians: stop waiting to live. Serve Christ now. He tells them to remain faithful in whatever situation God has called them. For married people, be faithful in marriage. For single people, serve God with undivided focus. For everyone, live content right where you are.

This is a radical message in a culture that says "you're incomplete until you do this or have that." Paul says you're complete in Christ now. A fireproof teen doesn't treat the present as a holding pattern — they build a fireproof life in the present.

Called Where You Are

Paul writes:

> "But as God hath distributed to every man, as the Lord hath called every one, so let him walk. And so ordain I in all churches" (1 Corinthians 7:17, KJV).

The Corinthian church was caught up in questions about relationships. Was it more spiritual to be single? Was marriage holier than singleness? Should believers try to change their status to be closer to God? Paul answers with a surprising word: stay where God has called you and walk faithfully there.

Notice Paul's language. He says God has "distributed" a place to each person. That means your situation in life is not random. Your family, your school, your stage of life, even your singleness or marriage—these are not mistakes. They are assignments from a wise God who knows what will shape you and where you can serve Him best right now.

This is where contentment comes in. Contentment doesn't mean pretending everything is perfect. It doesn't mean never longing for change. It means resting in the truth that God knows what He is doing with your life. Instead of thinking, "When I finally get a boyfriend, a driver's license, a job, then life will start," Paul says, "No—your life has already started. Serve Christ where you are."

Contentment:

Resting in God's plan instead of chasing something else.

Paul insists this is not just for Corinth but for "all churches." Contentment is not a side issue—it's part of discipleship everywhere. And it speaks directly to the restless heart of a teenager. Culture pushes you to believe that your value comes from milestones, achievements, or status updates. But Paul says your value comes from belonging to Christ. Whether single or dating, in middle school or high school, popular or overlooked—you are already called, already owned, already loved.

That's why Paul can call both singleness and marriage gifts. Each has its own opportunities and challenges, but neither makes you more or less spiritual. The question isn't, "What status will make me complete?" The question is, "Am I being faithful where God has placed me?"

Contentment doesn't mean passivity. It doesn't mean you can never change jobs, move towns, or one day marry. But it does mean you refuse to chase identity in those changes. You don't wait to glorify God until your situation improves—you walk faithfully in the place you are today.

So Paul's counsel to the Corinthians comes down to this: stop treating your status as the measure of your worth. Christ is your worth. Stop waiting for life to begin once circumstances change. Christ has already called you. Your job is to walk—step by step, faithfully reflecting Him in your current setting.

That is what it means to live content.

Key truths for teens:

1. **God Has You Where You Are on Purpose.** Your current situation isn't an accident. School, family, church, and community are your assignment right now.

2. **Singleness Is Not Second-Class.** Paul calls singleness a gift. It allows undistracted devotion to Christ. For teens, this means using your time now to grow in faith, skills, and service.

3. **Relationships Are Stewardships.** Marriage isn't a cure for loneliness or sin. Relationships don't complete you; Christ does. When the time is right, relationships are a trust from God, not an identity.

4. **Obedience Is More Important Than Status.** God doesn't rank people by their relationship status or social status but by their faithfulness.

5. **Stay Faithful Until God Moves You.** Don't live in constant discontent. Use your current stage as training ground for future service.

For teens today:

- Don't treat high school as "dead time."

- Don't wait for a relationship to start serving God.

- Develop habits of holiness and service now.

- See your worth in Christ, not in popularity or status.

- Trust God's timing instead of living in constant discontent.

Summary: Complete in Christ Now

- **God Calls You Where You Are:** Your current season is not an accident.

- **Singleness Is a Gift, Not a Gap:** Use it to grow and serve.

- **Relationships Are Not Identities:** They're trusts from God at the right time.

- **Faithfulness Beats Status:** God measures obedience, not milestones.

Paul's point: live fully for Christ in the present. Don't sit in the waiting room. Build now what will last forever.

Application: Practicing Contentment

1. See This Season as Training Ground. The habits you build now — prayer, Scripture, self-control, service — form your foundation for adulthood.

2. Stop Comparing Your Timeline. Some friends may date, others may get opportunities you don't. God's plan for you is personal.

3. Steward Your Time Wisely. With fewer adult responsibilities, you have space to learn, volunteer, develop skills, and deepen your walk with Christ.

4. Develop Godly Friendships. Choose friends who encourage your faith. Learn to relate to the opposite sex with respect and purity.

5. Focus on Character Over Romance. Rather than obsessing over dating, invest in becoming the kind of person who honors God in any relationship.

6. Trust God's Timing. He knows when and how to bring opportunities, friendships, and future partners into your life.

Practical ideas for teens:

- Write a "contentment gratitude list" of blessings in your current stage.

- Try a one-week "no-complaint" challenge about your circumstances.

- Ask a mentor what they wish they'd done with their teen years for Christ.

Ask yourself this week:

- Am I treating my life as a waiting room or a training ground?

- How can I serve God more fully right now?

- What lies have I believed about relationships or status?

Activities & Discussion

Icebreaker: Bring a wrapped gift labeled "Singleness" and another labeled "Marriage." Ask which one students would rather open first. Then explain Paul says both are gifts — the issue is how you use them.

Discussion Questions:

- Why does Paul tell believers to "remain in the calling" they're in?

- What's one blessing of being single as a teen?

- How can viewing singleness as a gift change your attitude?

- Why do we sometimes believe "life starts later"?

- How can we support each other in contentment?

Group Activity: Relationship Myths vs. Truth.

Make a list of common teen myths ("I need a boyfriend/girlfriend to be happy") and then debunk them with Scripture.

Unity Project: Encourage students to pray for each other's contentment and future.

Memory Challenge: Write 1 Corinthians 7:17 on the board and erase words gradually as students recite it.

Memory Verse

1 Corinthians 7:17 (KJV):

"But as God hath distributed to every man, as the Lord hath called every one, so let him walk. And so ordain I in all churches."

Leader's Note

Encourage students to memorize it and talk about "walking" in their current calling.

Prayer

"Lord Jesus, thank You for calling us where we are. Help us stop waiting to live and start serving You now. Teach us to see singleness as a gift, relationships as a stewardship, and faithfulness as success. Give us joy and contentment in this season and trust for the next. In Jesus' name, Amen.

Leader's Notes

- Illustration Idea: Use two jars — one labeled "waiting room" (sitting still), one labeled "training ground" (filling with weights or tools). Show the difference.

- Teaching Tip: Teens may feel left out or pressured. Emphasize dignity, not shame.

- Visual Aid: Draw a road labeled "Calling" with markers for different life stages. Emphasize faithfulness at each marker.

- Group Guidance: Handle questions about dating or marriage gently. Point back to identity in Christ.

- Memory Verse Drill: Ask each student to say one word of the verse in order, like a chain.

Session 9 – Freedom with Boundaries

Just Because You Can Doesn't Mean You Should

Imagine being given the keys to a sports car. No speed limits, no rules — at least that's what it looks like. You hit the gas. But soon you realize: there are other cars on the road. People crossing the street. Speeding recklessly puts everyone at risk.

Paul tells the Corinthians: you're free in Christ — but freedom comes with responsibility. They were arguing over eating meat offered to idols. Paul's point: even if it's technically allowed, you might choose not to if it harms a weaker believer.

For teens, this principle applies to music, media, habits, and social choices. Fireproof faith asks not "What can I get away with?" but "How can I glorify God and protect others?

Liberty, Love, and Conscience

Paul writes:

"But take heed lest by any means this liberty of yours become a stumblingblock to them that are weak" (1 *Corinthians 8:9, KJV).*

"Whether therefore ye eat, or drink, or whatsoever ye do, do all to the glory of God" (1 Corinthians 10:31, KJV).

Background:

In Corinth, almost every cut of meat you could buy had been part of a temple sacrifice. For some believers, it was no big deal. They knew idols weren't real, so why waste good food? But others had been rescued out of idol-worship. For them, eating that meat felt like going back to their old life.

Paul steps into the tension: Yes, you are free in Christ. But freedom doesn't mean doing whatever you want. True freedom means the ability to love. And love sometimes looks like setting your rights aside for the sake of someone else's spiritual health.

He says, "Knowledge puffeth up, but charity edifieth" (1 Corinthians 8:1). Knowing you can do something doesn't make it wise. Knowledge can inflate your pride; love builds up your brother or sister in Christ. Paul even goes so far as to say: if food makes my brother stumble, I'll never eat meat again (8:13). That's maturity—choosing sacrifice over self.

What This Means

This is one of the most practical chapters for teens today. It shifts the question from:

- "What am I allowed to do?" to

- "How does my choice affect others?"

Freedom in Christ is real. You're not under a rulebook of rituals to get to heaven. But freedom has boundaries—not because God wants to trap you, but because He wants you to love your neighbor.

For the Corinthians, it was about meat. For you, it might be music, movies, parties, social media, gaming, or even language. None of those things may be sinful in themselves, but how you use them matters. Your choice could either strengthen someone else's faith or trip them up.

Conscience

Paul introduces the idea of the conscience—that inner sense of right and wrong that God has given every person.

Consciences are not all at the same place. A newer believer might be bothered by something that doesn't trouble you. The mature response is not to mock them or pressure them, but to protect them.

> **Conscience**:
>
> The inner sense of right and wrong that helps guide your choices.

If Christ gave His life for your brother or sister, then your freedom should never become the reason they stumble. Love is more important than liberty.

The Glory of God

Paul sums it up in one sweeping sentence: "Whether therefore ye eat, or drink, or whatsoever ye do, do all to the glory of God." (10:31).

That's the real test for freedom: Does this glorify God? Does it reflect His goodness, His holiness, and His love? Or is it just about proving I can do what I want?

Living for God's glory doesn't mean life is small—it means every detail can shine with purpose. Eating, drinking, hanging out with friends, scrolling, listening to music, playing sports—every ordinary thing becomes a chance to reflect Him.

For Teens Today

Paul's words speak into a world where "You do you" is the anthem. Culture says freedom means no limits. Christ says freedom means responsibility. You don't ask, "What can I get away with?" You ask, "How can I build others up and honor God?"

That shift is what makes faith fireproof. Teens who learn this principle won't burn out chasing boundaries—they'll stand strong because their choices are anchored in love and aimed at God's glory.

Key truths for teens:

1. Freedom in Christ Is Real. You're not saved by rules. Christ set you free from sin and the law.

2. Freedom Is Not License. You can choose to limit yourself out of love. Christian maturity shows in self-control.

3. Love > Liberty. Paul says if eating meat makes his brother stumble, he'll never eat it again. That's the heart of Christlike love.

4. Conscience Matters. Not everyone's conscience is at the same place. Be patient with those who struggle.

5. Everything for God's Glory. Paul sums it up in 10:31 — whatever you do, do it for God's glory, not your ego.

For teens today:

• Not every movie, song, or party is wise.

• Your choices can shape younger believers' view of Christ.

• Ask not "What's wrong with it?" but "What's right about it?"

Summary: Mature Love Chooses Restraint

• Freedom Is a Gift: Christ set you free from sin and rule-keeping.

- Love Limits Liberty: You sometimes say "no" to protect others.

- Conscience Deserves Respect: Don't mock or pressure weaker believers.

- Glorify God in All You Do: Every choice can point to Christ.

Paul's point: Spiritual maturity isn't pushing boundaries but protecting hearts. Fireproof teens think about how their choices impact their friends and their witness.

Application: Using Freedom Well

6. Test Your Motives. Why do you want to do this? For fun? For status? For Christ?

1. Ask the Freedom Questions:

    A. Is it helpful?

    B. Is it loving?

    C. Does it glorify God?

D. Could it trip someone else up?

2. Model Restraint. Teens are bombarded with "Do what you want." Christ says, "Love your neighbor." Sometimes that means choosing not to watch, listen, or post certain things.

3. Respect Different Consciences. Some believers feel free about an issue you don't. Some don't. Walk humbly.

4. Teach Others by Example. Younger believers watch older ones. Show them a pattern of wise choices.

5. Remember the Goal: Freedom in Christ is freedom to serve, not self-indulge.

Practical Ideas for Teens:

- Create a "Freedom Checklist" with the four questions above.

- Fast from a non-essential (social media, soda, certain music) for a week to practice restraint.

- Discuss in small groups: what's an area where I might need to limit my liberty for love?

Ask yourself this week:

- Am I using my freedom to glorify God or myself?

- Is there a choice I make that could cause a weaker friend to stumble?

- What's one freedom I could voluntarily limit this week out of love?

Activities & Discussion

Icebreaker: Put a jump rope on the floor. Ask volunteers to see who can jump the "closest" without stepping on it. Show how focusing on the edge can lead to falling over. Connect to Christians who see how close to sin they can get.

Discussion Questions:

- What does Christian freedom mean to you?

- Why does love sometimes limit liberty?

- How can our choices be stumbling blocks to others?

- What's an example of a wise limit you've chosen?

- How can we glorify God in ordinary activities?

Group Activity: Freedom Debate.

Split into two groups. One argues "I'm free to…" The other argues "But love says…" Then discuss how to find balance.

Unity Project: Have students identify one area they can voluntarily limit to help a weaker friend (like avoiding a certain movie or app).

Memory Challenge: Write 1 Corinthians 10:31 on the board and erase words gradually as students recite it.

Memory Verse

1 Corinthians 10:31 (KJV):

"Whether therefore ye eat, or drink, or whatsoever ye do, do all to the glory of God."

Prayer

"Lord Jesus, thank You for setting us free. Teach us to use our freedom wisely. Help us love others more than we love our rights. Show us where to limit ourselves for Your glory and our friends' good. Make our choices a clear reflection of Your love. In Jesus' name, Amen."

Leader's Notes

Illustration Idea: Bring two items — one clearly harmful, one neutral but potentially distracting. Show the difference between sin and stumbling blocks.

Teaching Tip: Teens may think limits = legalism. Frame it as love and maturity.

Visual Aid: Draw two circles — "Freedom" and "Love" overlapping to make "Wisdom."

Group Guidance: Respect students at different stages of conscience. Don't shame them.

Memory Verse Drill: Have two teams recite alternating words of the verse to reinforce learning.

Session 10 – Worship That Honors God

Showing Up to the King's House

Imagine getting an invitation to visit the President or the King. You wouldn't show up late, distracted, or wearing pajamas. You'd come prepared, respectful, and focused because of who you're meeting.

Paul reminds the Corinthians that when they gather for worship, they're coming before the living God. But the Corinthians were turning worship into a party. Some were arriving drunk at the Lord's Supper. Others were pushing ahead of their brothers and sisters. Paul says: stop — worship is about Christ, not you.

Teens know what it's like to go through the motions in church — scrolling their phones, whispering to friends, thinking about lunch. Paul's words call us higher: worship is meeting with the King of Kings. Fireproof teens learn to approach God with reverence and joy, not boredom or distraction.

Reverence, Order, and Love

Paul writes:

> *"Let all things be done decently and in order"* (1 Corinthians 14:40, KJV).

The Corinthian Problem

The church at Corinth had a worship problem. Their gatherings weren't marked by reverence but by chaos. Some were speaking in tongues without interpretation, others were trying to teach at the same time, and still others were showing off their spiritual gifts in a way that confused rather than encouraged. Instead of building up the church, their meetings were tearing it down.

Paul reminds them that God is not the author of confusion but of peace (14:33). Worship is not about drawing attention to ourselves—it's about drawing attention to the Lord. That means approaching worship with respect, clarity, and order.

Reverence for the King

Think about it: if you were invited to stand in the throne room of a king, you wouldn't stroll in wearing pajamas, chatting loudly, or scrolling on your phone. You would come prepared, focused, and respectful—because of who you were meeting.

When we gather for worship, we are coming before the King of Kings. The same God who created galaxies, who

Worship:

The acknowledgement and acceptance of God's authority over your life.

thundered at Sinai, who spoke the universe into existence—He is the One we sing to, pray to, and hear from when His Word is read.

Worship is not a casual hangout. It is not background noise while we check our notifications. It is a holy moment in the presence of Almighty God.

What Reverence Looks Like

Paul's call for "decency and order" doesn't mean worship has to be stiff or lifeless. It means it should be purposeful, honoring, and clear. There is a time to sing with joy, a time to sit quietly, a time to listen, and a time to respond. When every part is done with intention, God's people are built up,

Reverence:

Showing deep respect and honor, especially in worship.

and outsiders can see that something real is happening.

Reverence shows up in practical ways:

- Coming prepared, not rushed or careless.

- Participating with focus, not distraction.

- Listening to God's Word as if your life depends on it—because it does.

- Singing as if you mean it.

- Treating prayer as a conversation with the living God.

For Teens Today

It's easy to slip into distraction during church. You might feel like checking your phone, whispering to a friend, or just zoning out. But when you do, you're acting like that kid in the throne room—surrounded by people honoring the King, while you're focused somewhere else.

Paul's words remind us: worship is not about us, it's about Him. When we remember who we are meeting, reverence becomes natural. We don't just show up—we show up ready, because we are stepping into the presence of the Lord of Glory.

Key truths for teens:

1. **Worship Is About Remembering Christ.** The Lord's Supper shows His death until He returns. Worship focuses our hearts on Jesus' sacrifice.

2. **Worship Is a Family Meal.** It's about unity. We come together as equals — rich or poor, popular or not.

3. **Preparation Matters.** Paul calls for self-examination before the Supper. Worship isn't a casual snack; it's a holy encounter.

4. **Disrespect Has Consequences.** Some Corinthians were "weak and sick" because of their irreverence. God takes worship seriously.

5. **Order Reflects God's Character.** Order and unity protect the church's witness. Teens learn that chaos and selfishness dishonor God.

For teens today:

- Worship is not a show but a sacred gathering.

- Your attitude, focus, and unity matter as much as the music.

- Preparing your heart before church changes everything.

Summary: Worship That Honors God

- Christ at the Center: Worship shows His death until He returns.

- Unity at the Table: We come as one family.

- Examine Your Heart: Prepare before you come.

- Honor the Moment: Order and reverence glorify God.

Paul's point: Worship is about Him, not us. Fireproof teens approach church like a royal appointment, not a casual hangout.

Application: Practicing Reverence and Joy

1. **Prepare Before You Arrive.** Pray on Saturday night. Get enough sleep. Ask God to open your heart.

2. **Participate Actively.** Sing, listen, take notes. Don't just spectate.

3. **Respect the Moment.** Put phones away. Stop side conversations. Focus on the words.

4. **Treat Others With Love.** Don't form cliques or ignore newcomers. Welcome everyone as family.

5. **Understand the Symbols.** The Lord's Supper isn't a snack; it's a sermon in symbols. Take it seriously.

6. **Make Worship a Lifestyle.** How you live Monday through Saturday affects your Sunday worship. Confess sin. Reconcile with others.

Practical ideas for teens:

- Keep a "Worship Journal" with sermon notes and prayers.

- Meet five minutes early to pray with a friend before youth group or service.

- Make a "no phone" pact with your group during worship.

Ask yourself this week:

- Am I approaching worship as a royal appointment or a routine?

- How can I help someone else feel welcome at church?

- What distracts me most during worship and how can I remove it?

Activities & Discussion

Icebreaker: Show two photos — one of a fancy banquet with place settings, one of a messy fast-food table. Ask: "Which picture looks more like our attitude toward church?"

Discussion Questions:

- Why does Paul emphasize remembering Christ in the Lord's Supper?

- How can teens prepare their hearts for worship?

- What are common distractions during worship, and how can we overcome them?

- Why is unity important when we gather?

- How can we show reverence without losing joy?

Group Activity: Worship Prep Challenge.

Ask each student to do one act of preparation this week before church (prayer, reading Scripture, arriving early). Share next session how it changed their worship experience.

Unity Project: Plan a "welcome squad" for your youth group — students who intentionally greet and include newcomers.

Memory Challenge: Write 1 Corinthians 11:26 on the board and erase words gradually as students recite it.

Memory Verse

1 Corinthians 11:26 (KJV):

"For as often as ye eat this bread, and drink this cup,

ye do shew the Lord's death till he come."

Leader's Note

Encourage students to memorize it and reflect on why we remember Christ's death until He returns.

Prayer

"Lord Jesus, thank You for inviting us to Your table. Forgive us for treating worship casually. Help us come with prepared hearts, loving unity, and joyful reverence. Let our worship honor You and show the world Your greatness. Teach us to remember Your death until You return. In Jesus' name, Amen."

Leader's Notes

- Illustration Idea: Bring two table settings — one elegant, one messy — to show attitudes toward worship.

- Teaching Tip: Teens may equate reverence with boredom. Emphasize joyful awe, not stiff formality.

- Visual Aid: Diagram of a table with Christ at the head and believers around it to show unity.

- Group Guidance: Use this session to talk about how your youth group approaches communion or worship services.

- Memory Verse Drill: Have students recite the verse in pairs, alternating words.

Session 11 – Gifts That Build, Not Break

The Team Without Roles

Picture a basketball team where everyone insists on being the star scorer. No one rebounds, no one defends, no one passes. It's chaos. The scoreboard tanks because no one is doing their role.

Paul tells the Corinthians: the church is like a body or a team. Every part has a role. When everyone tries to be the star or show off a flashy gift, the whole body suffers.

Teens often feel like they have nothing to offer in church. Or they see church as a stage for the "gifted" people up front. Paul says every believer matters. God gave you a role. The goal isn't showing off — it's building up.

One Body, Many Members

Paul writes:

> *"But the manifestation of the Spirit is given to every man to profit withal"* (1 Corinthians 12:7, KJV).

> *"...seek that ye may excel to the edifying of the church"* (1 Corinthians 14:12, KJV).

Paul steps in and reminds them: spiritual gifts don't exist to inflate your ego. They exist to strengthen the team. He writes, "But the manifestation of the

Manifestation:

The visible or practical evidence of the Spirit's work.

Spirit is given to every man to profit withal" (1 Corinthians 12:7, KJV). Gifts aren't handed out at random. The Spirit distributes them with care so that the whole body benefits. A gift misused for self-promotion is like a player hogging the ball—flashy but destructive. A gift used in love builds others and keeps the church's scoreboard moving in the right direction.

Paul goes deeper with his famous body analogy. The eye can't say to the hand, "I don't need you." Neither can the head dismiss the feet. Every part matters, even those less visible. Teens today feel this pressure acutely. Our culture celebrates the stage presence, the viral video, the social-media influencer. But in Christ's church, the quiet encourager, the faithful servant, and the consistent prayer warrior are just as necessary as the one with public gifts. Without them, the body limps. With them, the body thrives.

The Corinthians ranked their gifts like trophies. Paul tells them that ranking was foolish, because the same Spirit empowers them all. The Spirit doesn't play favorites. He equips some to teach, some to lead, some to serve, some to give, some to show mercy, and some to evangelize. Each one matters. In fact, Paul reminds them that God often honors the gifts that look less glamorous. Just like a basketball team needs defense and rebounding more than one more ball hog, the church needs hidden servants more than one more showman.

At the same time, Paul sets boundaries. Gifts aren't meant to turn worship into chaos. That's why he adds in chapter 14: "...seek that ye may excel to the edifying of the church" (v.12, KJV). The test of a gift isn't "Was it exciting?" but "Did it build others up?" Corinth had confused energy with edification. Paul says real worship requires clarity, order, and love. A dozen people shouting in different languages at once might look spectacular, but it leaves the church confused. One person teaching with clarity builds everyone.

> **Edification:**
>
> To build up, strengthen, or encourage someone in their faith.

Paul will spend the next chapter (13) showing that even the most spectacular gift is worthless without love. He gives the "cymbal crash" example to prove that without love, gifts become noise. We'll dive deeply into that next time. But for now, he lays the groundwork: love must govern gifts, or else gifts will divide instead of unite.

So what does this mean for teens? It means stop trying to be the star scorer. Ask instead: what role has the Spirit given me to strengthen my team? Maybe you're not on stage, but you are the one who notices when someone is hurting. Maybe you don't lead the group, but you make sure no one is left out. That is the Spirit at work. A fireproof church isn't built on one superstar gift; it is built on every member knowing their role, serving in humility, and loving enough to put the team ahead of themselves.

Key truths for teens:

1. **Every Believer Has a Gift.** You're not an accessory. God gives each Christian at least one gift to build others.

2. **Gifts Are for Serving, Not Showing Off.** They "profit withal" — they're for the whole group, not your reputation.

3. **Some Gifts Were Temporary Sign Gifts.** Tongues and interpretation, healing, and prophecy were given in the early church to authenticate the apostles and establish the gospel. Once Scripture was complete,

these sign gifts ceased. Today we focus on service, teaching, encouragement, giving, leadership, mercy, etc.

4. **Love Is Greater Than Any Gift.** Paul puts Chapter 13 between 12 and 14 to show that without love, gifts mean nothing.

5. **Order Protects the Church's Witness.** Paul insists on understandable speech and self-control. Confusion dishonors God.

For teens today:

- You have real gifts to use now, not "someday."

- Flashy isn't always spiritual.

- Love and clarity trump hype.

Summary: Gifts for Building, Not Showing

- **One Body, Many Gifts:** Everyone matters.

- **Given to Profit All:** Gifts exist to help others grow in Christ.

- **Sign Gifts Were Temporary:** Tongues and similar gifts confirmed the message in the early church.

- **Love and Order Rule:** Without them, gifts become noise.

Paul's point: Fireproof teens discover their gifts and use them humbly to strengthen the body of Christ, not to build their own platform.

Application: Discovering and Using Your Gifts

1. Believe You're Needed. God has something for you to contribute. Don't sit on the bench.

2. Discover Your Service Area. Ask: What do I enjoy doing for God? What do others affirm in me? This often points to your gift.

3. Start Small and Faithful. Gifts grow with use. Help in nursery, greet at the door, assist with tech, write encouragement notes.

4. Focus on Service Gifts. Today God calls us to gifts like teaching, encouragement, giving, leadership, mercy, helps — not sign gifts.

5. Practice Love as the Context. Serve with humility, not self-promotion.

6. Respect Others' Gifts. Don't envy or despise differences. We need each other.

Practical Ideas for Teens:

- Take a simple spiritual gifts inventory focused on service gifts.

- Ask a leader where you can help once a month.

- Write down three ways you could build someone up this week.

Ask yourself this week:

- Am I a builder or a spectator at church?

- How can I use my time and talents now?

- Do I value love and clarity over hype?

Activities & Discussion

Icebreaker: Hand out slips of paper with different "roles" (eye, hand, foot, ear). Ask students to act them out silently. Then ask what happens if a body only has one part. Connect to 1 Corinthians 12.

Discussion Questions:

- Why does Paul compare the church to a body?

- What's the danger of making flashy gifts the focus?

- How does knowing some gifts were temporary help us focus today?

- What gifts can teens use right now to build the church?

- How does love make your gift powerful?

Group Activity: Gifts Map.

Draw a body outline on a whiteboard. Have students write their names in areas where they feel gifted (hands = service, mouth = teaching, ears = listening/ encouragement). Show how each part matters.

Unity Project: Pair students to pray for each other's gifts and service opportunities during the week.

Memory Challenge: Write 1 Corinthians 12:7 on the board and erase words gradually as students recite it.

Memory Verse

1 Corinthians 14:12 (KJV):

"...seek that ye may excel to the edifying of the church."

Prayer

"Lord Jesus, thank You for giving us gifts to build Your church. Forgive us for envy or pride. Show us how to serve with humility, clarity, and love. Protect us from chasing hype. Help us use our time, talents, and energy to strengthen others and glorify You. In Jesus' name, Amen."

Leader's Notes

Illustration Idea: Bring a puzzle missing pieces. Show how one missing piece leaves the picture incomplete.

Teaching Tip: Teens may be curious about tongues. Clearly explain cessation in age-appropriate language: "Those gifts were signposts; now we have the full map — Scripture."

Visual Aid: Draw a team roster or body diagram to show roles.

Group Guidance: Encourage students to try service opportunities and reflect on what energizes them.

Memory Verse Drill: Form a circle and have each student say one word of the verse to complete it.

Session 12 – Love: The Greatest Gift

The Noisy Cymbal

Picture a marching band where one player refuses to stop clanging the cymbals. The music is drowned out, the melody lost, and everyone covers their ears. Paul says that without love, even the most impressive gifts sound like "a sounding brass, or a tinkling cymbal."

Teens today are encouraged to "stand out" and "be the best." But Paul flips the script: better to serve in obscurity with love than to shine without it. Fireproof teens learn that love — agape love — is what makes any gift, any action, any life truly valuable.

Agape love isn't a mood. It's a decision to act for another's good, even at cost to yourself. That's what Christ did for us. That's what makes the church fireproof.

Caption

The Supremacy of Love

Paul writes:

> *"Though I speak with the tongues of men and of angels, and have not charity, I am become as sounding brass, or a tinkling cymbal. ... And now abideth faith, hope, charity, these three; but the greatest of these is charity" (1 Corinthians 13:1, 13, KJV).*

The Corinthian church was fascinated by gifts. Speaking in tongues, prophecy, knowledge, even faith that could move mountains — these became status symbols. Members compared and competed, measuring spirituality by how spectacular someone appeared. The result was noise and division. Into this confusion, Paul does something surprising. He doesn't ban gifts. He doesn't dismiss them as worthless. Instead, he pauses the conversation and says, "Let me show you a better way." That "more excellent way" is love.

Paul opens with a shocking claim. Imagine speaking every language on earth — and even angelic speech. Imagine having prophetic insight so sharp you could explain mysteries that baffle the wisest scholars. Imagine faith so strong you could pray mountains into the sea. Imagine giving away your possessions to the poor or even offering your body in sacrifice. All of that, Paul says, without love, equals nothing. It's like a cymbal crash that drowns out the music — loud, impressive, but empty.

Why? Because love is the essence of Christ's character. Gifts are temporary and partial. Love is eternal and complete. Prophecy will end. Knowledge will fade. Tongues will cease. But love never fails. In fact, Paul says love outlasts even faith and hope. Faith will one day become sight. Hope will one day be fulfilled. But love will continue forever because it reflects the eternal nature of God Himself.

Paul then describes love with verbs, not adjectives. Love isn't simply a feeling; it is action. Love suffers long. It chooses patience when wronged. Love is kind — it takes initiative to do good. Love does not envy, parade itself, or puff up with pride. Love doesn't behave rudely, demand its own way, or fly into quick anger. Love doesn't keep a mental scorecard of offenses. Instead, it rejoices in truth, bears burdens, believes the best, hopes even in hardship, and endures through trials.

For teens today, Paul's description cuts against the grain of culture. Love isn't shallow romance or temporary friendship that fades when it's inconvenient. Love is steady, selfless, and sacrificial. It doesn't use people; it serves them. It doesn't seek applause; it seeks another's good. And while spiritual gifts may look flashy, love is what makes them meaningful. A teen who sings beautifully in church but is cruel to classmates is like a cymbal drowning out the song. A teen who quietly serves a younger sibling or welcomes the new kid at school reflects Christ more than one who hogs the spotlight.

Paul isn't belittling faith or hope — both are essential. But he reminds the Corinthians, and us, that love is the greatest. It is the glue that holds the body together, the motive that keeps gifts from turning into pride, and the mark that shows the world we belong to Jesus. Without it, all else is noise.

Key truths for teens:

1. Love Is Greater Than Gifts. You can be talented, smart, or popular — but without love it's empty.

2. Love Is Sacrificial, Not Selfish. Agape love acts for another's good, even when it costs you.

3. Love Is a Choice, Not a Feeling. Patience, kindness, humility — all are decisions empowered by the Spirit.

4. Love Outlasts All Else. Prophecies, tongues, and knowledge will vanish. Love endures forever.

5. Love Is the Mark of Maturity. The real sign you're growing in Christ isn't a gift — it's love.

For teens today:

- Social media can measure likes, not love.

- Real friendships thrive on patience, forgiveness, and sacrifice.

- Love distinguishes Christ's followers from the world.

Summary: The More Excellent Way

- Love Makes Gifts Matter. Without love, you're just noise.

- Love Is Patient and Kind. Not jealous or proud.

- Love Never Fails. Everything else fades, but love remains.

- Love Is the Greatest Proof of Christ.

Paul's point: Fireproof teens measure their lives not by talent or clout but by sacrificial, agape love.

Application: Living Agape Love

1. Redefine Love God's Way. Love isn't "how someone makes me feel" but "how I choose to treat them."

2. Practice the 1 Corinthians 13 Checklist. Before responding to someone, ask: Is my reaction patient? Kind? Humble?

3. Love Hard People. Anyone can love their friends. Agape love shines when you love the difficult, the awkward, the overlooked.

4. Forgive Quickly. Love "keeps no record of wrongs." Release grudges to God.

5. Serve Secretly. Do acts of kindness no one sees. This trains your heart to love, not impress.

6. Ask the Spirit for Power. We can't manufacture agape love ourselves. We must let Christ live through us.

Practical Ideas for Teens:

- Each day this week, pick one person to show sacrificial love to.

- Make a "Love Inventory" of how patient, kind, humble you've been — not to shame but to grow.

- Write down the names of people you struggle to love and pray for them daily.

Ask yourself this week:

- Who is God calling me to love sacrificially right now?

- How can I show kindness instead of irritation?

- How can my social media reflect agape love?

Activities & Discussion

Icebreaker: Bring a metal pot and spoon. Bang it loudly and then softly. Ask: "How pleasant is this sound?" Read 1 Corinthians 13:1.

Discussion Questions:

- Why is love greater than gifts or achievements?

- How does Paul describe love's actions (1 Cor. 13:4–7)?

- What's the hardest part of that description for you?

- How can you practice sacrificial love in your school or family?

- How does agape love reflect Christ's character?

Group Activity: Love in Action.

Brainstorm as a group: "What would it look like if our youth group lived 1 Corinthians 13 at school?" Make a short list of actions and pick one to try this week.

Unity Project: Pair students to encourage each other daily with a kind message or prayer this week.

Memory Challenge: Write 1 Corinthians 13:4–7 on the board and erase phrases as students recite it.

Memory Verse

1 Corinthians 13:13 (KJV):

"And now abideth faith, hope, charity, these three; but the greatest of these is charity."

Leader's Note

Encourage students to memorize it and talk about why love outranks everything else.

Prayer

"Lord Jesus, thank You for loving us with perfect, sacrificial love. Teach us to love others as You have loved us. Make our lives more than noise – fill us with patience, kindness, and humility. Help us love even when it costs us. Let Your agape love flow through us daily. In Jesus' name, Amen."

Leader's Notes

- Illustration Idea: Bring a heart-shaped box but fill it with noise-makers instead of candy to show gifts without love.

- Teaching Tip: Teens can confuse love with approval or attraction. Clarify agape love as sacrificial action.

- Visual Aid: Draw three columns labeled Faith, Hope, Love with Love in bold at the top.

- Group Guidance: Challenge students to put 1 Corinthians 13:4–7 into their own words and use it as a daily filter.

- Memory Verse Drill: Have each student say one trait of love aloud in a circle.

Session 13 – Unshakable Hope: The Power of the Resurrection

The End of the Story

Think of your favorite movie or book. If you already know the ending is happy, you watch the scary parts differently. You don't panic when the hero's in danger because you know how it ends.

Paul tells the Corinthians: because Jesus rose from the dead, we know how our story ends. Death doesn't win. Fear doesn't get the last word. Everything we do for Christ matters forever.

For teens, this changes everything. Anxiety about the future, pressure to fit in, fear of missing out — all lose power when you know Christ has conquered death and guaranteed eternal life. Fireproof teens live with courage and purpose now because they know how the story ends.

Christ Has Risen, We Will Rise

Paul begins this chapter with the heart of the Gospel:

> *"For I delivered unto you first of all that which I also received, how that Christ died for our sins according to the scriptures; and that he was buried, and that he rose again the third day according to the scriptures" (1 Corinthians 15:3-4, KJV).*

Notice the weight Paul places here. This isn't just background information. This is the core. Without the resurrection, the Gospel collapses. If Jesus stayed in the grave, sin would not be defeated, death would not be conquered, and faith would be in vain. But Christ did rise, bodily, historically, on the third day, just as Scripture promised. That truth anchors everything we believe and everything we live for.

Paul then calls Jesus the "firstfruits":

> *"But now is Christ risen from the dead, and become the firstfruits of them that slept"* (1 Corinthians 15:20, KJV).

The "firstfruits" were the first part of the harvest, offered to God as a guarantee of more to come. Christ's resurrection is that guarantee for us. Because He lives, all who belong to Him will live. His empty tomb is the down payment on our future resurrection. For the Corinthians, this was meant to silence doubts about whether the dead would rise. For teens today, it means death isn't the end of your story. Christ's victory over the grave is your victory too.

But Paul doesn't stop with hope for the future. He draws a direct line from the resurrection to our life right now:

"Therefore, my beloved brethren, be ye stedfast, unmoveable, always abounding in the work of the Lord, forasmuch as ye know that your labour is not in vain in the Lord" (1 Corinthians 15:58, KJV).

Because the resurrection is true, nothing done for Christ is wasted. Serving when no one notices, resisting temptation when no one thanks you, standing for truth when it costs you friends, choosing purity when culture mocks you — none of it is in vain. Without the resurrection, suffering is meaningless. With the resurrection, suffering becomes investment. Every act of faith, every sacrifice of love, every hidden labor counts forever.

This is the "spoiler" that changes everything. The resurrection tells us how the story ends — Christ victorious, death defeated, His people raised in glory. So teens don't have to be ruled by anxiety, pressured into compromise, or paralyzed by fear of missing out. Fireproof teens can live courageously and purposefully now, because they know the ending is already written. And it is good.

Key truths for teens:

1. **The Resurrection Proves the Gospel.** If Christ didn't rise, your faith is worthless. But He did rise — your sins are forgiven, your hope is sure.

2. **Christ Is the Firstfruits.** Like the first sheaf of grain guaranteeing the harvest, Jesus' resurrection guarantees ours.

3. **Death Doesn't Have the Last Word.** Paul calls death "the last enemy." Christ defeated it. Teens don't have to fear it.

4. **Your Labor Is Not in Vain.** Because of the resurrection, nothing done for Christ is wasted. School, chores, service, witness — all count forever.

5. **Resurrection Hope Shapes Present Living.** It fuels purity, courage, and perseverance. We can stand firm because our future is secure.

For teens today:

- Overcome anxiety with the hope of eternal life.

- Live boldly because Christ has conquered your biggest fear.

- See your daily choices as investments in eternity.

Summary: Hope That Holds

- **Christ Rose:** Your faith is real, your sins forgiven.

- **We Will Rise:** Death is defeated, the future is secure.

- **Stand Firm Now:** Because of the resurrection, you can be unshakable.

- **Nothing Is Wasted:** Every act of faithfulness matters forever.

Paul's point: Fireproof teens live with unshakable hope — a hope that changes how they handle pressure, temptation, and fear today.

Application: Living Resurrection Hope

1. Let the Resurrection Define Your Identity. You're not defined by failure or popularity but by Christ's victory.

2. Let the Resurrection Shrink Your Fears. Death is the biggest fear; Christ defeated it. Smaller fears lose their grip.

3. Invest in What Lasts. Since your labor is not in vain, serve, study, and witness with joy. Every small act for Christ echoes in eternity.

4. Persevere Through Hardship. Knowing the end of the story gives you courage in trials. Don't quit when it's hard.

5. Purify Your Life. 1 John 3:3 says whoever has this hope purifies himself. Live like you're headed for eternity.

Practical Ideas for Teens:

- Journal three fears and write "Jesus rose" over them.

- Do one act of service this week because it's "not in vain."

- Memorize 1 Corinthians 15:58 and repeat it before tests or stressful situations.

Ask yourself this week:

- How does believing Christ rose change my daily life?

- What fear do I need to surrender to resurrection hope?

- Where can I "abound in the work of the Lord" today?

Activities & Discussion

Icebreaker: Bring a sealed envelope labeled "Ending." Give students a suspenseful mini-story on paper, but don't show the ending until after reading. Then reveal the ending. Discuss how knowing the ending changes how you experience the story.

Discussion Questions:

- Why is the resurrection essential to the gospel?

- How does Christ's resurrection guarantee ours?

- What does 1 Corinthians 15:58 mean for your school or home life?

- How can resurrection hope help with anxiety or peer pressure?

- What's one area of your life you'd live differently if you truly believed "nothing is wasted"?

Group Activity: Not in Vain Chart.

Have students list things they do in a week. Mark which ones are "work of the Lord" and talk about how to infuse each with eternal purpose.

Unity Project: Pair students to pray for each other's courage to live resurrection hope.

Memory Challenge: Write 1 Corinthians 15:58 on the board and erase words gradually as students recite it.

Memory Verses

1 Corinthians 15:58 (KJV):

"Therefore, my beloved brethren, be ye stedfast, unmoveable, always abounding in the work of the Lord, forasmuch as ye know that your labour is not in vain in the Lord."

Prayer

"Lord Jesus, thank You for dying for our sins and rising again. Fill us with unshakable hope. Help us stand firm, live pure, and abound in Your work knowing it's not in vain. Replace our fears with courage and our apathy with purpose. Let our lives point to Your victory. In Jesus' name, Amen."

Leader's Notes

- **Illustration Idea:** Bring a "paid in full" stamp or a trophy — show how Christ's victory guarantees ours.

- **Teaching Tip:** Teens may see resurrection as distant. Tie it to current anxieties, hopes, and purposes.

- **Visual Aid:** Timeline from "Cross" to "Resurrection" to "Future Resurrection" showing our hope anchored in history.

- **Group Guidance:** Encourage honest talk about fears or doubts. Offer pastoral support and Scripture.

- **Memory Verse Drill:** Recite 1 Corinthians 15:58 in unison as a rallying cry.

Session 14 – Standing Firm and Finishing Well

The Finish Line

Picture a marathon runner. They've trained for months. The race is long, exhausting, and filled with obstacles. The crowd cheers at the start, but by mile 20 the field is thin. The prize goes not to the fastest starter but the faithful finisher.

Paul ends 1 Corinthians with a rallying cry: "Watch ye, stand fast in the faith, quit you like men, be strong. Let all your things be done with charity" (16:13–14, KJV). He's calling believers to endurance — to keep the faith, stay alert, and do everything in love.

Teens often start strong in faith but drift as pressures mount. Paul's closing words give us a blueprint to finish well. A fireproof teen doesn't just burn bright for a season — they keep the flame alive for a lifetime.

Paul's Closing Charge

Paul writes:

> *"Watch ye, stand fast in the faith, quit you like men, be strong. Let all your things be done with charity" (1 Corinthians 16:13-14, KJV).*

Paul closes his letter with a rapid-fire series of commands that sound like a coach giving final instructions before the big game: "Watch ye, stand fast in the faith, quit you like men, be strong. Let all your things be done with charity" (1 Corinthians 16:13–14, KJV). After all the correction, encouragement, and teaching in this letter, he doesn't end with a lecture. He ends with a charge.

"Watch ye." The word means stay alert. A runner who loses focus stumbles. A soldier who falls asleep at his post puts the whole unit at risk. In Corinth, danger was everywhere: false teachers, temptations, pride, division, and persecution. Paul says: keep your eyes open. For teens today, the dangers look different — distraction, comparison, compromise, and doubt — but the call is the same. Watch. Be alert to what's pulling you away from Christ.

"Stand fast in the faith." Don't drift. Don't cave. Don't let the ground be taken from under your feet. The Corinthians had wavered — excusing sin, arguing over leaders, doubting the resurrection. Paul tells them to plant both feet firmly in the Gospel they had received: Christ died, was buried, and rose again. Teens face daily pressure to bend — to blend in, to stay silent, to go along. Paul's words are clear: plant your feet in the truth of God's Word and don't budge.

"Quit you like men." That old phrase simply means, "Act with courage." It doesn't mean be macho; it means be mature, responsible, and brave. Corinthian believers were acting like spiritual children — selfish, quarrelsome, and easily swayed. Paul tells them: grow up. Courage is not the absence of fear; it is doing the right thing even when fear whispers in your ear. For a teen, that might mean speaking up for someone being mocked, resisting a temptation when friends push, or holding to biblical conviction in a culture that laughs at it.

"Be strong." Not in your own willpower, but in the Lord. Strength here isn't about muscles or personality; it's about spiritual stamina. The marathon illustration fits perfectly: the prize goes not to the fastest starter but to the faithful finisher. Paul knows the race is long. He knows the last miles are the hardest. That's why he tells the Corinthians: keep pressing forward in Christ's strength.

But then Paul ties it all together with one final command: **"Let all your things be done with charity."** Without love, all the watching, standing, courage, and strength can become harsh, proud, or cold. Love keeps the guardrails in place. Love turns strength into service. Love makes courage gentle and watchfulness compassionate. Paul never lets us forget: the Christian life isn't about winning arguments or proving toughness. It's about finishing the race in Christ's strength, and doing everything with His love.

For teens, these words are both challenge and encouragement. The Christian life is not a sprint. It's a marathon. You'll face moments when the crowd has gone home, when your legs ache, when quitting feels easier. But the Spirit who raised Jesus from the dead is the same Spirit who gives you strength to finish. Keep watching. Keep standing. Keep running. And whatever you do, let love mark every step. That's how you finish well.

Key truths for teens:

1. Watch Spiritually. "Watch ye" = stay alert. Don't drift. Pay attention to your spiritual life. Like a lifeguard scans the waves, a believer watches for temptation and opportunities.

2. Stand Fast in the Faith. Know what you believe. Stand on Christ as your foundation. Don't be swayed by trends, peer pressure, or false teaching.

3. Quit You Like Men (Act Courageously). This old phrase means "act like grown-ups." Be courageous, take responsibility, and lead in integrity.

4. Be Strong. Strength isn't arrogance but endurance. Keep going when it's hard.

5. Do Everything in Love. Strength without love becomes harshness. Love without strength becomes weakness. Paul ties all together: courage and love, truth and grace.

For teens today:

- Life after high school will test your foundation.

- You'll need to stay alert, courageous, and loving in college, at work, online.

- Finishing well starts with daily faithfulness now.

Summary: The Fireproof Life in Four Commands

- **Watch:** Stay alert to temptation and opportunity.

- **Stand Fast:** Hold firmly to the faith and to Christ.

- **Be Courageous and Strong:** Live boldly and endure hardships.

- **Do Everything in Love:** Let love guide every action.

Paul's point: Fireproof teens are future fireproof adults. They're not playing at faith; they're training to finish well.

Application: Training for the Finish

1. **Daily Watchfulness.** Have a spiritual "check-in" each day — Scripture, prayer, self-examination. Ask: Where am I drifting? Where can I grow?

2. **Strengthen Your Core Beliefs.** Know what you believe about Christ, Scripture, and salvation. This helps when you face challenges in college or culture.

3. **Practice Courage Now.** Stand up kindly but firmly for your faith at school. Integrity in small choices trains you for big ones.

4. **Build Endurance.** Commit to consistent church attendance, prayer, service. Little habits add up to resilience.

5. **Lead With Love.** Being strong doesn't mean being harsh. Combine conviction with kindness.

Practical Ideas for Teens:

- Create a "Finish Well Plan" — three habits you'll commit to for the next month.

- Memorize 1 Corinthians 16:13–14 as your rally cry.

- Journal your biggest fear about the future and write a prayer of courage.

- Make a gratitude list of mentors who've modeled finishing well.

Ask yourself this week:

- Am I building daily habits that will last beyond high school?

- Where do I need courage right now?

- How can I combine strength and love in my relationships?

Activities & Discussion

Icebreaker: Set up a mini relay race. Each student carries a baton labeled with one of the four commands ("Watch," "Stand," "Strong," "Love"). Discuss how each step leads to finishing well.

Discussion Questions:

• What does it mean to "watch" spiritually?

• Why is it important to "stand fast" before challenges come?

• How can teens practice courage in daily life?

• Why must everything be done in love?

• What habits help you finish well instead of burning out?

Group Activity: Fireproof Commitments.

Review all 14 sessions. Ask each student to write one takeaway from each and assemble a "Fireproof Life Plan."

Unity Project: Pray over each student's "Finish Well Plan" as a group, laying hands on shoulders if appropriate.

Memory Challenge: Write 1 Corinthians 16:13–14 on the board and erase words gradually as students recite it.

Memory Verse

1 Corinthians 16:13-14 (KJV):

"Watch ye, stand fast in the faith, quit you like men, be strong. Let all your things be done with charity."

Leader's Note

Encourage students to make this their life verse for the year.

Prayer

"Lord Jesus, thank You for walking with us through this journey. Help us watch, stand firm, be strong, and do everything in love. Make us fireproof for life – not just today but for decades to come. Help us finish well, holding fast to You until we see You face to face. In Jesus' name, Amen."

Leader's Notes

- **Illustration Idea:** Bring an actual baton or a medal to symbolize finishing well.

- **Teaching Tip:** Teens need to see that finishing well is built on daily choices, not one dramatic moment.

- **Visual Aid:** Timeline from Session 1 to Session 14 with milestones.

- **Group Guidance:** Encourage ongoing mentorship and accountability after this study ends.

- **Memory Verse Drill:** Recite the verse as a "pledge" together at the close of the program.

FIREPROOF
COMMENTARIES

About Fireproof Commentaries

Fireproof Commentaries are the distillation of Pastor James Burke's decades of preaching, teaching, and shepherding God's people. Written from the pulpit rather than the ivory tower, each volume combines clear biblical exposition with practical, Christ-centered application. The series equips pastors, teachers, and believers to understand Scripture deeply and apply it faithfully, helping local churches stand firm in faith and unity. Whether used for sermon preparation, small-group study, or personal devotion, Fireproof Commentaries are designed to build "fireproof" churches that endure cultural pressures and internal challenges by staying rooted in God's Word.

www.ingramcontent.com/pod-product-compliance
Lightning Source LLC
Chambersburg PA
CBHW082248120626
46555CB00009B/3007